The Call Home

poems by
Susan Johnson

A Publication of The Poetry Box®

Poems ©2023 Susan Johnson
All rights reserved.

Editing & Book Design by Shawn Aveningo Sanders
Cover Design by Shawn Aveningo Sanders
Cover watercolor painting by Dylan Johnson
   based on photograph by Jeremy Hynes
Author Photo by Doug Johnson

No part of this book may be republished without permission from the author, except in the case of brief quotations embodied in critical essays, epigraphs, reviews and articles, or publisher/author's marketing collateral.

ISBN: 978-1-956285-34-5
Printed in the United States of America.
Wholesale distribution via Ingram.

Published by The Poetry Box®, April 2023
Portland, Oregon
https://thepoetrybox.com

*There's a thread you follow. It goes among
things that change. But it doesn't change.*

—William Stafford

Contents

- 7 | Along Scatter Creek
- 8 | 1952
- 9 | Iodine
- 11 | Womanchild
- 13 | On the Banks of the Teanaway River
- 14 | After Your Funeral Mass
- 15 | First Snowfall
- 16 | When Nothing's To Be Done
- 18 | On Your Birthday
- 19 | To My Daughter
- 20 | Home after Six Years Grandmothering in Seattle
- 21 | To My Aunt
- 22 | Like This
- 23 | In Time We Know
- 24 | The Ninth Month
- 25 | This I Know
- 26 | Above the River
- 27 | One May Morning
- 28 | And Now
- 29 | In Every Direction
- 30 | Psalm 29
- 31 | When What You Have Left Is Loss
- 32 | Teach Me

- 35 | Acknowledgments
- 37 | Early Praise for *The Call Home*
- 39 | About the Author

Along Scatter Creek

The pebble in the brook secretly thinks itself a precious stone.
—Japanese Proverb

And aren't we each a pebble,
stone broken long ago,
one piece of great formation,
purified in mountain melt,
ground by glacier flow,
tumbled, rushed into eddies,
under rapids, shaped, polished,
magnified in water, jewel among
jewels, as light as the weight of god?

1952

In the officers' quarters at Camp Lejeune,
on the edge of the grass, under thickness of hedge,
in softness of shadow, I knew wilderness,
was certain I could stay forever.

I tied my broomstick horse to the water spigot,
crouched through brambles of green in search of a friend
I'd found the day before, pulsing along spines of branch,
tuft of black, band of brown, wooly bear caterpillar.

From the pocket of my sundress, I pulled the string
I'd snipped from tangle in the kitchen drawer.
With the sureness of my mother's hands braiding my hair,
I wound the string behind his head into a loose leash.

I guided him through rocks and roots,
his furriness focused on me with quiet attention,
away from cries of the baby, reign of my sisters,
echoes in the empty well of my father's absence.

You know, I loved that caterpillar and he loved me.
I slipped the leash over his head and we lay still,
breath to breath, eye to eye,
first communion on consecrated ground.

Iodine

*The element of iodine
was once used as a disinfectant.*

Her mother kept a brown bottle
in the medicine drawer.
The round odor of purple stain,
the cool tip of glass wand,
the confidence in her mother's song,
calmed the injuries of childhood.

*When heated, iodine evaporates
into a beautiful violet vapor.*

Her father loathed the color violet,
called her a tart at twelve
when she posed with a friend
in purple pants and a peasant top.
She exchanged those clothes
for a blue plaid skirt and white shirt
like her uniform at Catholic school.

Her mother discovered her kissing a boy
"just like the squirrels in broad daylight."
She watched herself evaporate,
vanish in the heat of her mother's anger.

*Iodine solutions were eventually replaced
by antiseptic agents that sterilize effectively.*

Her mother eventually
replaced the brown bottle
with hydrogen peroxide
and isopropyl alcohol.
They kept her clean,

[. . .]

sterilized effectively,
never tempted her to trip and fall.
She avoided the injuries of adolescence
though she longed for the
earthy waft of purple stain.

Womanchild

My mother snapped a dampened dress from the laundry bag,
sculpted the sleeves around the curve of the padded ironing
    board,
pressed each cuff with steamy precision,
and listened to my fourth-grade stories
as I stretched my full body across the wooden floor,
chin propped in palms, eyes on every glide of the hot iron.

She was my star in our motherdaughter stories:

Rooting herself on the front stoop, baseball bat in hand,
peeping Tom prowling our neighborhood.

Racing through stop lights, pressing police,
one hand on the steering wheel, one on my bloody eye
ripped ragged from an errant swing.

But then, there was that first kiss — Freddie Williams,
eighth-grade voltage at the front door after school.

I would change that story:

Not   *damnit to blue hell get in the house.*
Not   *just like the squirrels in broad daylight.*
Not   *banished to the nuns.*

My mother would just unlatch the door,
whisper a welcome, shelter me,
narrate the holiness of touch,
escape the shame seeded in one kiss.

I would dampen my fiery years,
hidden in the anger of Holden Caulfield,
desperate in the dreams of Woodstock,

[. . .]

lonely with friends who could not know me,
lonely for her.

I would change the ending:

It would be the two of us and
the curve of her kitchen table,
my baby asleep for a morning nap,
breakfast dishes stacked in the drying rack,
Formica counters cleared, coffee strong —
black like she taught me.

We would speak as mother, daughter, woman,
watch cardinals congregate at her feeder,
sun mirror itself on river,
recall the ironing board and stories we'd lost.

But since we did not have that ending, I have another:

Morning warble of welcome,
mountain bluebird calls from pine
just outside my door. I pray her name,
settle like a child on a wooden bench.
We unlatch forgiveness.
I tell her all my stories again.

On the Banks of the Teanaway River

Mountain bluebird lightens the pines,
snowfields let go their winter hold,
churn brown in roiling crests,
bear blackened branches of
charred trees to final rest.

You have lifted beyond our knowing,
summon our sorrow to rise with you
while your song drifts down
from green of needled branches
from the trembling throats of birds.

After Your Funeral Mass

~1~

After your funeral Mass,
after friends emptied the house,
the salty tides of the Chesapeake
slid, silent, along the Rappahannock.

Blackbird perched on glass door
sill, peered into the room at us.
Back and forth she paced, all day,
for a week. We knew.

~2~

Today, my mountain home, far
from any salty water. In a box
nailed high on cedar siding,
a chorus of nestlings cries out.

Mother nuthatch hurries to them,
one insect in her beak, swoops to sky,
returns, all day. Insect by insect,
she answers their helpless need.

First Snowfall

The children chased first flakes,
caught them on the tongue, and
hard winter ground muted to soft.

Now, thirty degrees, frozen rain
glistens the snow to shimmery, and
the children glide along the glassy

sheen while aspens, a neighborhood
of silvery skins, a congregation, assemble
to celebrate the sacraments:

children,
snow, rain,
gleam of ice.

When Nothing's To Be Done

*I left you that day with your friend
in a cabin along the shore of the lake.
I would sail with my friend —
a few hours, not long — then pick
you up and take you home.*

The clank of trailer chains rattled
as the boat slid from the ramp
out to swell of snowmelt waters,
cold spray against my cotton pants.
Wind thrummed through cedars,
reluctance through me, as I climbed
to the canvas of the catamaran.

He raised the sail — a thunderous flap,
then we sped from the gravel beach, he
loosened the ropes to control the thrust,
and we rushed through tattered waves.

We lurched in zigzags, cabins
on shore shrinking from sight.
His eyes flashed surprise.
Mine locked shut.

One wild gust flung us to water,
bodies and sails slapping, mast
plunging to dark below, hulls
upturned — a drifting beetle.
We struggled, chilled, too far
from shore to swim, too muted
by wind to be heard,
the water too cold.

We couldn't slow light fading that day
or shorten shadows dimming the beach.
We finally ran out of ideas, of hope.
When nothing's to be done,
there's nothing. A certain peace
settled on me. We drifted.

*Out of the deepening twilight
a vision of you arose,
drifted before me
above the waves,
called to me for help.*

Your mother, that moment
knew to live.

A shout—sudden from shore—
then the whine of a motorboat
pierced the wind, grew near, and
kindness welcomed us aboard.
We abandoned the carcass
drifting in darkness, found
grace in a stranger's face.

On Your Birthday

There's a thread that binds
a mother, this mother,
to a daughter, my daughter, you.

A thread strong as spider's silk
secures us from any height,
stretches across wide spaces,

branch to branch, beam to beam,
nourishes us, nests the young,
lifts us from danger, practically invisible,

durable as steel in rough wind,
shimmery in sunlight,
spun on demand.

To My Daughter

You do not have to be good.
                    —Mary Oliver

You do not have to be brave.
You can show your grief
like vine maple flaming
her loss on mountain slopes.
She knows this sorrow.

It is all right to weep as you lay
the children to bed, to long,
to dwell in disappointment,
like swallow in her loss to crow,
her eggs small and helpless.

I remember when you called out
to moon. You were two years old.
Come down moon, come down.
And she did not answer,
and you cried and called again,

and she did not answer,
and you cried and called again,
and she did not answer,
and you cried and I took you up
and carried you home.

Is it moon now who pulls your womb?
Will she empty you, will she heal you?
Go ahead and cry, dear one,
go ahead while your baby birds
rest in their beds.

Home After Six Years Grandmothering in Seattle

My heavy boots crunch
along the icy trail, an April thaw,
straight into a sudden blast
of morning snow squall.

Below the pines, balsamroot.
Pale green clusters, soft
arrow spears, hold steady
in the confusion of snow.

Patient, they guard their swelling
buds, tiny folded yellow petals,
hidden sunbursts, unhurried,
willing to wait for May.

The bitter wind halts as swiftly
as it rose. Snow gives way
to warmth. So too, my body,
braced from the cold, loosens,

my pace slows, my bones quiet.
The quickened pulse of city
sifts from me like feathers
drifting to the forest floor,

to pale leaves, to waiting buds.
Home again on timbered trails,
I recall the nearly forgotten,
reliable tug of gravity.

To My Aunt

I have tried to love you.
I have phoned you, consoled you,
sent kitchen towels, school pictures,
canned jams for Christmas and birthdays,
known you are lonely, flown home each year,
heard stories from crumbling
albums of family photographs.

But since we never talked of him,
since my mind still freezes in fear
when I see his face framed
on your walls, and since,
when you mention his name,
I go mute,
I know I have not loved you,

for when I—a child—told,
your icy silence exiled me
to the back rooms of family.

Because you never spoke of it,
because after he died you softened,
because you loved my children and so
tried on affection, clumsy, awkward,
because . . . because . . . because . . .
because we never spoke of it,

and death drifts near you now,
some raw grief concealed beneath
the gloss of giftwrap erupts,
a box of rotted fruit, trapped
acid of failed love. And so
I go to you, your final days,
and pray to learn to love you.

Like This

There is a time for sorrow —
my mother's early death,
my brother's,
a friend lost to cancer,
my nephew to a needle.
There is a time to know deep
woundedness, to taste suffering.

There are moments, too, like this —
when some pure note sings as we
sit to talk on the wooden bench
beside the door to the post office,
when the weight of worldly
trouble is lightened for a bit.
Do you feel it?

I can tell by the way our eyes
lock, our ease in conversation,
how you relax against the wooden
back, how I lean a little toward you.
I can tell by the way our words spill
out like soft rain on wildflowers —
gentle, regenerative, true.

We watch while neighbors walk
in, walk out — mailbox keys,
packages, hellos. They know.
We see it in their glances, hear
it in hellos — their loss, their joy —
like ours, carried together.
And isn't that a kind of love?

In Time We Know

Love spins a silken thread, then
stretches it, a kindly warp that
steadies us across this mortal loom.
In birth. In death. In days between.

And Suffering weaves a weft
of coarsened yarn, shuttled
through those glossy threads.
To cross. Recross. Over. Under.

And thus in time we know
the two have bound us whole —
a rough and lovely cloth.

The Ninth Month

Our oldest granddaughter, expecting
her first, prepares her nursery. Clean
sheet on clean crib, diapers stacked
in four columns, tidy on the shelves.

Two drawers store carefully folded
cotton blankets, newborn gowns.
Ten tiny headbands the family
made hang in a row on the wall.

She rocks in a wooden chair,
one hand on a child's book,
one on her fullness:
> *Goodnight room*
> *Goodnight moon*
> *Goodnight cow*
> *jumping over the moon**

Wildflowers bloom a month
early, then dry and wither in heat.
Aspens shed their still-green leaves.

Baby stirs in her womb
at the sound of her voice.

California burns. Alaska,
Canada burn. Washington,
Idaho, Oregon burn.

Four fires ignite to the north.
Helicopter thrums overhead.
She shuts the nursery window
as smoke seeps through the screen.

*from *Goodnight Moon*, Margaret Wise Brown

This I Know

Today, on a walk to the river,
my granddaughter plucked two
Oregon grapes from clusters
near the trail. We giggled,
our tongues bitter blue.

We watched the salmon
drift in clear and shallow
waters—slow, weary,
nest-diggers, scales
scraped white.

The dead, their skins
translucent as ghosts,
haunted the stretch
of river's edge as far
as we could see.

This I know:
the salmon dead,
a thousand eggs,
the jade green current,
blue stain on a child's hand.

Above the River

The moon waxes toward solstice.
We find our way above the river
with an old and certain ease,
through lupine and paintbrush,
the brilliant orange of tiger lily.
Processions of cow parsnip line the trail.
Our breath, exhalation of forest.

Piles of broken cones cover
a trailside bench — squirrel work.
Pileated woodpecker taps nearby.
Snake slides away through brush.
Inch-high fir seedlings reach toward
a cloudless June sky. A shower
of cotton drifts from swollen pods.

Here, a young snowshoe hare lies so still
in the curve of a tree root, eyes open,
fur perfect, smooth, we think at first
she is alive. Coyote disappears ahead.
He will return. Our talk — the family,
a birth, a death, a wedding. Rush
of river below — a chant, a prayer.

One May Morning

After the ash of wildfire
shrouded firs on the ridge,
after it seared our lungs,

after a hurricane seized Puerto Rico,
after a mudslide took your friend,
after cancer took your aunt,

before we were millions sick,
before we witnessed murder
by an indifferent knee,

we planted new carrots
in the garden, one tiny
seed at a time, and

you found a brown caterpillar,
lonely in green of chard, and
you cradled her wooliness

in your tiny hands, and
built a cardboard home,
spread leaves across the floor,

poured water into saucers,
propped open a door, and
sang her a quiet song.

And Now

There is silence in the sap of an old
pine, silence that holds our morning
prayer. There is silence that holds you
apart from me as we walk the river trail.

There is silence in the luminescence
of moon, and a silent first flame
of wildfire. There was silence that
held our babies' first breaths,

and the silent hole in my father's last.
And now this silence in the freeze
of first frost and the pitiless
persistence of your silent disease.

In Every Direction

In every direction the whine
of chain saw, thud of falling trees.
Elk calves cry out, huddle
among withered huckleberries,

above salmon skins haunting
the banks of the shallow river.
Black bear rips apart the neighbor's trash,
claws the gate from our compost heap,

begs through the night,
her only light the dim spark
of stars silenced behind aimless clouds.
Yesterday, a small doe climbed

our wooden stairs, hungry for ash
berries scattered across the steps.
Her young watched her from the yard.
I watched her through the window,

both of us stunned, silent,
for a full moment, still.

Psalm 29

Love's voice echoes over the oceans and seas.
— Nan Merrill

In the plentiful fields of lupine
    and sage,
in the wild sweep of clouds
    in the west,
in the song of red-winged blackbird
    in the brush,
Love's voice echoes in the hush
    between us
on the meandering trail
    along this swollen hill,
in the tender truth
    that summons us,
assuring us,
    reassuring us,
that an unguarded heart
    is the only way.

When What You Have Left Is Loss

*This great unknowing
is part of their holiness.*
  —Denise Levertov

Sit with the trees,
don't talk,
smell the dank
musk of leaf rot,
say thank you,
kiss the ground.

Breathe with the trees,
still your mind,
pray like a child,
like a cloud,
like a bird,
like a leaf.

Teach Me

On the edge of the water with the patience of sap,
you wait in stillness, for flicker of fish, glint of frog.
With timeless wings you rise in slow flight,
the call to home, your colony in cottonwood.

Heron, please teach me.
Teach me patience to know my needs are met.
Teach me grace to rise with love.
Teach me purpose to serve community.
Teach me stillness to hear the voice of god.
Teach me quiet consent to the call home.

Acknowledgments

I offer grateful acknowledgment to the editors of these publications where the following poems first appeared, sometimes in different forms:

Cirque Journal: "Along Scatter Creek," "Iodine," and "Womanchild"

Earth's Daughters: "To My Aunt"

Raven Chronicles: "On the Banks of the Teanaway River"

The Shrub-Steppe Poetry Journal: "After Your Funeral Mass," "To My Daughter," "Like This," "In Time We Know," "This I Know," "One May Morning," and "Teach Me"

WA 129+: "When Nothing's To Be Done"

WA Poetic Routes: "Home After Six Years Grandmothering in Seattle"

Windfall: A Journal of Poetry and Place: "The Ninth Month"

Yakima Coffeehouse Poets: "1952" and "Above the River"

Thank you to my family, of all generations, for the lessons of love that guide me.

Thank you to my mentors and to my companion poets who have supported and encouraged me. You ground me, inspire me, and stretch me.

Many thanks to my loving husband, Doug, for your steadfast, patient presence in reviewing any draft I bring to you at any time. Your love of language and keen insight feed my poems.

Praise for *The Call Home*

Susan Johnson's poems call us home in the best of ways, back to our rightful place in the natural world, back to the simple hopes and joys of life, like planting *new carrots/ in the garden, one tiny/ seed at a time.* With the wisdom of a sage, she crafts poems that showcase the saving grace of small moments, how they can redeem even our darkest hours, teaching us that *an unguarded heart/ is the only way.*

—James Crews, author
of *Kindness Will Save the World:
Stories of Compassion & Connection*

Susan Johnson writes with grace and gracefulness about family, nature, even pain and horror. Her poems glow with an almost holy sense of nostalgia and forgiveness, sometimes sad, always gentle. Accessible and engaging, Johnson's book is a finely crafted antidote to the world right now.

—Susan Blair, author of *What Remains of a Life*,
editor of *The Shrub-Steppe Poetry Journal*

The poems in Susan Johnson's *The Call Home* ask us to pay attention to the human relationships in our lives, particularly family. For good or ill, those relationships matter. If good, we revere them. If painful, we must understand and forgive. Again and again, the poems turn to the healing powers of the natural world in times of trial. In the closing poem, "Teach Me," from which the title is drawn, the poet encounters a blue heron in the wild and asks: *Heron, please teach me./ Teach me patience to know my needs are met./ Teach me grace to rise with love./ Teach me purpose to serve community./ Teach me stillness to hear the voice of god./ Teach me quiet consent to the call home.* Another poem, "In Time We Know," uses weaving as a figure to conjoin Love and Suffering: *And thus in time we know/ the two have bound us whole—/ a rough and lovely cloth*. Actually, that metaphor could apply to the book as a whole: a tapestry of words bespeaking pain, love and much, much wisdom.

—Ed Stover, author of *Homecoming*,
President, The Yakima Coffeehouse Poets

The Call Home goes deep, revealing Susan Johnson's love of the truth and her need to tell it. Brave, vulnerable, and willing to explore—even if what she finds is difficult—Johnson offers a religion of noticing things, a spirituality of paying attention. *Look at this* she says to us, pointing out things that go on in the world: Look at this broomstick horse tied to a water spigot. Look at this hot iron glide, pressing *each cuff with steamy precision*. At these new carrots planted *one tiny seed at a time*. Look as wildfire threatens, *as smoke seeps through the screen*. Look at grief drifting down *from green needled branches, from the trembling throats of birds*.

These poems are intimate, raw, moving, and in moments, willfully hopeful. You'll find things you need in this searching collection: clarity, heartbreak, simplicity, tenderness, joy, strangeness, beauty, loss. And you'll discover some things about forgiveness, about learning to love one another, even when it's hard.

Rich in feeling, profound in insight, these are poems you will remember long after closing the book.

—Terry Martin, author of *Wishboats*,
The Secret Language of Women, and *The Light You Find*

About the Author

Susan Johnson writes in the mountain town of Roslyn, Washington, where she has lived with her husband and their children for over forty years. She hikes daily with family and friends on trails along the Cle Elum River Valley. As a spokeswoman for a Roslyn citizens' group, she worked with others to promote sustainable forestry and to protect wildlife habitat. Susan taught in the local schools and university and held leadership roles in state and national writing initiatives. She was named the 2009 Washington State Teacher of the Year.

Susan is grateful to be active in a vibrant poetry community. Her work has appeared in *Cirque Journal: A Literary Journal for the North Pacific Rim, Earth's Daughters, Poetic Shelters, Poets Unite! LiTFUSE @10 Anthology, Raven Chronicles, Rise Up Review, The Shrub-Steppe Poetry Journal, WA129+, Washington Poetic Routes, Windfall: A Journal of Poetry of Place,* and *Yakima Coffeehouse Poets.*

About The Poetry Box®

The Poetry Box, a boutique publishing company in Portland, Oregon, provides a platform for both established and emerging poets to share their words with the world through beautiful printed books and chapbooks.

Feel free to visit the online bookstore (thePoetryBox.com), where you'll find more titles including:

Tracking the Fox by Rosalie Sanara Petrouske

Elemental Things by Michael S. Glaser

Listening in the Dark by Suzy Harris

In Transit by Teddy Norris

Signs by Emily Newberry

Our Aching Bones, Our Breaking Hearts by Joel Savishinsky

Soundings by David Gonzalez

The Weight of Clouds by Cathy Cain

This Is the Lightness by Rachel Barton

Earthwork by Kristin Berger

The Round Whisper of No Moon by Peter Kaufmann

Tell Her Yes by Ann Farley

My Husband's Eyebrows by Leanne Grabel

Sophia & Mister Walter Whitman by Penelope Scambly Schott

A Nest in the Heart by Vivienne Popperl

and more . . .

www.ingramcontent.com/pod-product-compliance
Lightning Source LLC
LaVergne TN
LVHW050029080526
838202LV00070B/6986